A GROSS INTRODUCTION

Grossology is everywhere—all over your body and all around you. Every single day you encounter gobs of disgusting things. Most of the time you don't even think about it. With the information in this book, you can finally embrace the grossness that surrounds you.

This book will set you on a path of icky knowledge that you can happily share with your family, your friends, your teacher, your neighbor. Anyone who will listen! Or maybe they won't want to listen, but you can tell them anyway.

What are you waiting for? Turn the page and start getting gross!

TABLE OF CONTENTS

6

DISGUSTING NOISES

BARF

A LONGER, MORE POLITE WORD FOR *BARF* IS *REGURGITATE.* "WHERE IS THE BATHROOM? I HAVE TO REGURGITATE."

- Have you ever gotten really sick and barfed a whole bunch? Did you notice your abdominal muscles got sore? That's because ralphing works out your abs.

- The word *nausea* comes from the Greek word *nausia*, for seasickness.

- For some people, just hearing someone puke makes them want to hurl.

SPIT

SPIT DOES SO MANY THINGS: IT WETS FOOD TO HELP YOU SWALLOW; KILLS CAVITY-CAUSING BACTERIA; TURNS STARCH LIKE BREAD INTO SUGAR; HELPS YOU TO TASTE THINGS; AND IT ALLOWS YOU TO MAKE SPIT BUBBLES.

- Urea and uric acid (basically pee) are found in saliva. So, that means that everyone has a pee pee mouth.

- Over your lifetime, you will make enough saliva to fill a large swimming pool, more than 25,000 quarts.

- An adult tongue has about 10,000 taste buds hanging out on it.

10

BURP

IT IS HARD TO BURP WHEN YOU ARE LYING ON YOUR BACK.

- Lying on your stomach while resting on your elbows helps air escape from your stomach. *Buuuurp!*

- In some cultures, burping after a meal tells the cook how much you enjoyed the meal.

- Fatty foods seem to make people belch more. "Good cheeseburger! *Burp.*"

- Sleeping on your side helps gas escape from your stomach. So, you can burp while you snore.

FART

ONE THIRD OF ADULTS HAVE METHANE GAS IN THEIR FARTS. METHANE GAS IS FLAMMABLE.

- Two of the chemicals—indole and skatole—found in stinky farts are used in perfumes! When those chemicals are diluted, they stop smelling yucky and start to smell quite nice.

- Farts produced by eating plant matter have little odor—with a few exceptions, like cauliflower, broccoli, and brussels sprouts, that release sulfur-containing compounds. Farts produced by eating meats and eggs smell the worst!

- You fart about fourteen times every day.

14

SNEEZE

ONE SNEEZE CAN SPRAY 100,000 SNOT DROPLETS INTO THE AIR.

- A sneeze can reach speeds of thirty-six miles per hour. Winds at this speed are called near gale winds.

- The sneeze droplets can travel almost twenty-seven feet! The snot droplets land on everything in their path.

- Germs from a sneeze can live on hard surfaces for up to twenty-four hours.

BODY GROSSNESS

SKIN

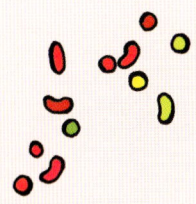

THE LARGEST ORGAN IN YOUR BODY IS YOUR SKIN. AN AVERAGE ADULT'S SKIN COVERS MORE THAN EIGHTEEN SQUARE FEET IF ALL SPREAD OUT AND WEIGHS ABOUT SEVEN POUNDS.

- Your skin is home to 1.5 trillion (1,500,000,000,000) micro-creatures. That is more than all the people who have ever lived on planet Earth!

- Over 1,000 different types of bacteria live on your skin.

- No matter how hard you scrub your face, you can never get rid of all the bacteria. Don't worry; they don't hurt you.

NOSE

WHEN YOU CRY, TEARS DRAIN INTO LITTLE HOLES IN THE SIDE OF YOUR NOSE. WHEN YOU CRY REALLY HARD, THE TEARS GUSH OUT OF YOUR NOSE AS WELL AS YOUR EYES.

- Your nose can smell best when you are between eight and ten years old. That's probably why kids notice gross smells faster than adults.

- In most people, one nostril is bigger than the other!

- Did you know that your nostrils take turns inhaling? You breathe more through one nostril than the other for three to four hours and then switch sides.

- The nose flute is an instrument played with the nose. Nostril air is blown through the flute to play notes. Do you think nose flute players borrow one another's instruments?

- As you age, your nose begins to sag, so it looks like it is getting bigger.

19

BLOOD

YOUR BLOOD GOES THROUGHOUT YOUR ENTIRE BODY MORE THAN 1,000 TIMES EVERY DAY.

- If you took all of the blood vessels in your body and laid them end to end, they could wrap around planet Earth TWICE.

- You could line up 7,000 red blood cells around the edge of a penny.

- An adult body makes about two million new red blood cells every second!

- Did you know, an average adult's body contains ten pints of blood? That's like thirteen soda cans of blood.

- Red blood cells live for only about three months because while traveling through the blood vessels, they get bumped and battered a lot.

SWEAT

TINY SWEAT GLANDS ALL OVER YOUR SKIN SQUIRT LIQUID WHEN YOU GET HOT. WHEN THE SWEAT SUCKS UP BODY HEAT, IT CHANGES TO A GAS, OR EVAPORATES. THE EVAPORATING SWEAT COOLS YOU DOWN.

- When you exercise, you can lose one quart of sweat an hour!

- You don't have any sweat glands under your fingernails or toenails.

- Sweat doesn't smell bad until skin bacteria munch on it to make it stinky.

ZITS

WHEN A PORE ON YOUR SKIN GETS CLOGGED WITH DEAD SKIN CELLS, SKIN OIL OR SEBUM, BACTERIA, AND BACTERIA WASTE, YOU GET THE MAGIC FORMULA FOR A ZIT.

- One zit is a pimple. A bunch of zits is acne.

- Around 90 percent of all teenagers get acne at some point.

- People of all ages can get acne, even babies in the womb. This is called perinatal acne.

- The yellow stringy thing that comes out of a blackhead when you squeeze it is actually dried grease.

- The word *acne* comes from the ancient Greek word *aknē*, meaning "eruption on the face." Seems zits have been around for a very long time.

KISSING

THERE ARE MORE BACTERIA IN YOUR MOUTH THAN THERE ARE PEOPLE LIVING IN THE UNITED STATES.

- You get more germs from someone by shaking hands than you do by kissing.

- You burn about .012 calories every time you peck someone on the cheek.

- Mononucleosis is a viral disease often called the kissing disease. Yes, you can get it from kissing, but you can also get it from sharing a glass, utensils, or food with someone who has the virus.

BLUSHING

WHEN NERVES TELL YOUR BLOOD VESSELS TO OPEN WIDE SO THAT BLOOD RUSHES IN, YOUR SKIN TURNS RED OR YOU BLUSH.

- Scientists do not know why we blush, but humans are the only animals that do it.

- When you blush, your stomach lining blushes, too.

- A fear of blushing is called erythrophobia.

- When some people blush, only their face turns red; for other people, their face, neck, and chest turn red.

STINKY FEET

- Each of your feet makes about 1/4 cup of sweat every day.

- Foot sweat does not make your feet stink—it is the sweat-eating bacteria that die and poop and pee on your feet that makes them oh-so-stinky.

- If you don't want your feet to stink, don't wear shoes. Or just wash your feet regularly.

31

BOOGERS

BOOGERS ARE MADE WHEN SNOT MIXES WITH DUST, DIRT, POLLEN, POLLUTION, SMOKE, OR ANYTHING THAT FLOATS IN THE AIR. WHEN THE SNOTTY CLUMP DRIES UP, A BOOGER IS FORMED.

- Seven out of ten people admit to picking their nose.

- Do you practice rhinotillexis? In Latin, *rhino* means "nose" and *tillexo* means "picking habitually." Yep, this is the medical word for nose picking.

- Boogers come in many colors. Yellow and green are the most common. However, they can be brown, black, purple, and orange! It depends upon the color of the dust that you breathed in.

34

CAVITIES

BACTERIA IN YOUR MOUTH LOVE TO EAT SUGAR AND SUGAR FROM STARCH. THEIR ACID WASTE DRIBBLES ONTO YOUR TEETH AND DISSOLVES THEM TO MAKE CAVITIES.

- Until 1938 the bristles of toothbrushes were made from pig hairs. After that nylon was used.

- The hardest substance in your body is tooth enamel.

- In Roman times, pee was used in toothpaste and as a mouthwash.

HAIR

HAIR IS ACTUALLY MADE OF DEAD CELLS.

- Hair traps smells. That is why hairy parts of your body get stinky.

- Each hair on your head grows about 1/100 of an inch every day.

- An eyelash lives for around 150 days.

PUTRID KITCHENS
EATING

EVER SPEW MILK FROM YOUR NOSTRILS? YOUR LITTLE UVULA SWINGS UP WHEN YOU SWALLOW TO STOP FOOD FROM GOING UP YOUR NOSE. SOMETIMES IT DOESN'T WORK IF YOU LAUGH AS YOU SWALLOW.

- The scientific word for chewing is *mastication*. Wouldn't it sound weird if your grandma said, "Now dear, masticate your food well"?

- The big scientific word for swallowing is *deglutition*. Seems easier to just say *swallow*.

- Smell and taste go together. If you have a stuffed-up nose, your food has less taste. If you smell something nasty while eating, your food may not taste as yummy.

YUMMY FOOD

A NIBBLE OF CHEESE COULD CONTAIN MORE BACTERIA THAN THERE ARE PEOPLE LIVING ON PLANET EARTH.

- Gelatin, which is used in some fruit snacks, is made by boiling animal skin, tendons, knuckles, and bones in water. Think of that the next time you enjoy a gummy.

- Some hot dogs can contain ground-up cow lips.

- A glass of water contains about 20,000 living creatures. Gulp!

41

TOILET

WHEN YOU FLUSH, A REALLY FINE PEE PEE MIST FLOATS OUT OF THE TOILET AND LANDS ON EVERYTHING IN THE BATHROOM. BETTER PUT YOUR TOOTHBRUSH IN A CUPBOARD OR DRAWER.

- Recycled toilet water is used to water golf courses and highway landscaping. It is ALMOST clean.

- Annual toilet races take place at Hampdenfest in Baltimore, Maryland. Each vehicle must contain a toilet. Teams consist of a driver, a pusher, and a crew member. The defecation vehicle that crosses the finish line first wins a trophy!

- The number of germs on your fingertips doubles after using the toilet—unless you wash your hands.

TOILET PAPER

- Some cultures don't use toilet paper; they use water or their hands.

- Before there was toilet paper, or paper even, people used straw, leaves, corncobs, and even clamshells to wipe.

- Toilet paper on rolls was invented in 1879 by the Scott brothers.

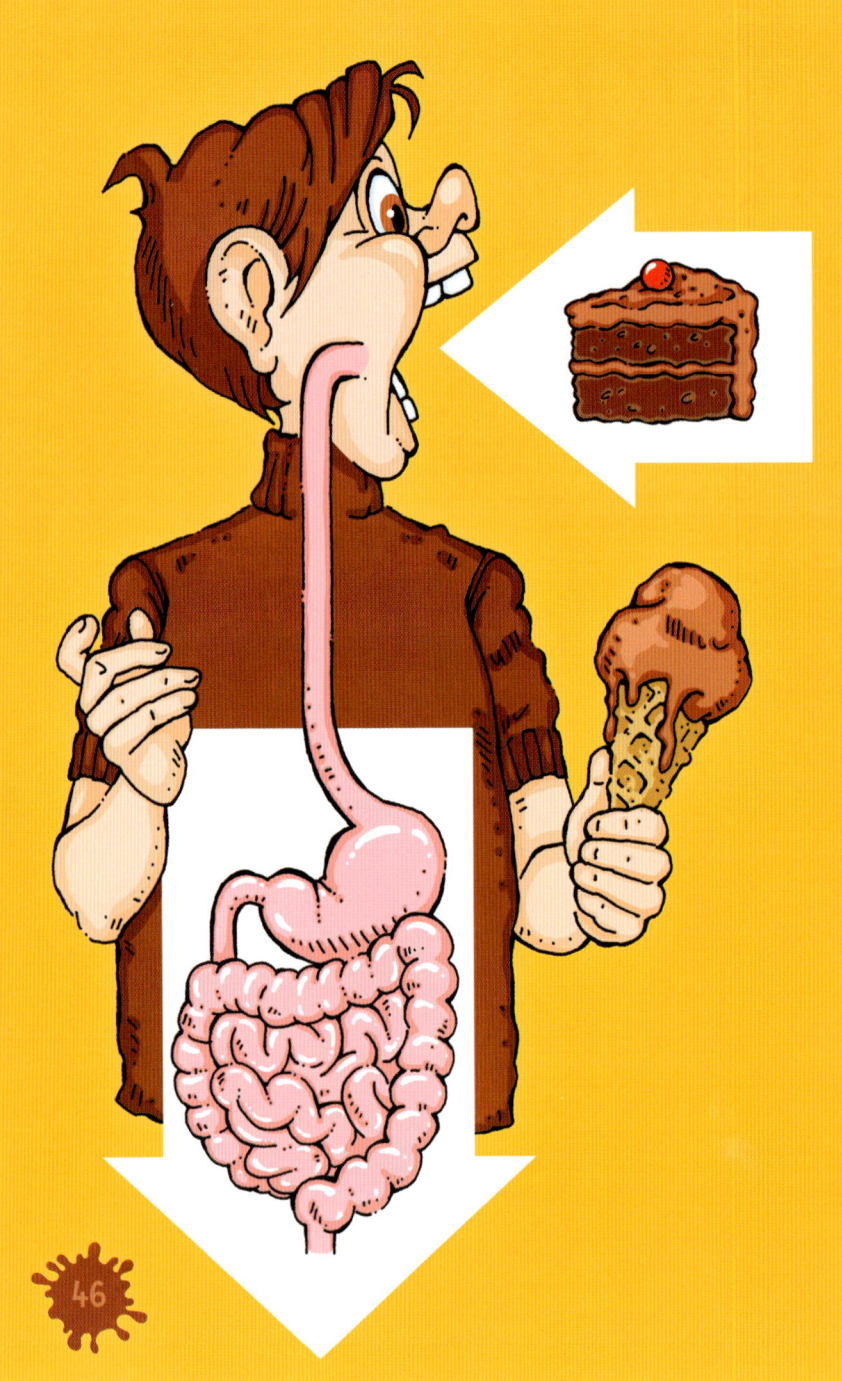

POO

A BIT OF POO THE SIZE OF A CHOCOLATE-COVERED RAISIN CAN CONTAIN 100 BILLION LIVING MICRO-CREATURES. THAT IS MORE LIVE CRITTERS THAN THERE ARE PEOPLE LIVING IN IN THE WORLD—TIMES TWELVE! IMAGINE A WHOLE POOP!

- Your small intestine is about four times longer than you are tall.

- The average adult in the United States eats almost a ton of food a year—all that food sure makes a whole lot of poop!

- If you squeezed out all of the bacteria from your intestines, you could almost fill up a coffee mug. Anyone want a sip?

PEE

THE AVERAGE PERSON PASSES 9,020 GALLONS OF URINE IN THEIR LIFETIME, OR ENOUGH TO FILL 315 BATHTUBS.

- Nocturnal enuresis is very common in young children—even you! Don't get all worried, though. Nocturnal enuresis is just bedwetting.

- *Micturition* is a medical word for peeing. So, you can tell your friends, "I gotta micturate."

- In the morning, you probably have as much as a pint of pee pee stored up.

50

DEODORANT

THE WORD *DEODORANT* COMES FROM TWO LATIN WORDS: *DE*, WHICH MEANS "AWAY," AND *ODŌS*, WHICH MEANS "SCENT."

- Roll-on antiperspirants work on about 40 percent of the sweat glands that you put it on. The rest just keep squirting sweat.

- If your brother has really stinky feet, you might suggest he put antiperspirant on his feet. Or maybe someone else can tell him.

51

52

HANDWASHING

HALF OF ALL MEN AND ONE QUARTER OF ALL WOMEN *DO NOT* WASH THEIR HANDS AFTER USING THE TOILET.

- Germs can live on unwashed hands for up to three hours.

- Right-handed people usually wash their left hand better, and left-handed people wash their right hand better.

- Between two million and ten million bacteria live between your fingertips and your elbow.

BABY POO

A BABY'S FIRST POO IS BLACK OR DARK GREEN AND VERY TAR-LIKE.

- After they start drinking milk or formula, their poo looks like yellow mustard or peanut butter. Yummy.

- In the first year of your life, you probably went through about 2,500 diaper changes. Whole lot of pooping going on.

- Babies in the womb are covered in fine hair called lanugo that goes into the fluid surrounding the babies. The babies swallow the hairs and poop out this first meal after they are born.

DOGS

DOGS SNIFF ONE ANOTHER'S BUTTS. THE SCENT GLANDS ON THE SIDES OF THEIR BUTTHOLES REVEAL HEALTH, SOCIAL POSITION IN THE DOG WORLD, AND WHAT WAS FOR DINNER.

- Ever catch your dog doing the carpet scrape wiggle? Rover is not dancing; he is scratching anal glands that may become clogged.

- Coprophagy. Dogs do it. Coprophagia is poop eating.

- Puppy breath smells different from adult dog breath. This icky, interesting breath will last for about six months or until your dog gets permanent teeth.

KITTY CAT

- Cats clean themselves by licking. Some hair gets pooped out, but some stays in the stomach and clumps up. So, they barf it out—hairballs!

- You can buy kits to help teach your cat to do its business in the toilet! You can't teach them to flush afterward, though.

- Cat poo can contain a parasite called *Toxoplasma gondii.* If the parasite infects rodents, it takes over their brains and makes them attracted to cats and cat pee.

- About sixty million people in the United States are infected with this cat-dookie parasite. Some people get a disease called toxoplasmosis, so pregnant women and people with immune diseases should not clean the litter box.

59

DUST MITES

HOUSE DUST IS ACTUALLY COMPOSED OF 70 PERCENT DEAD SKIN CELLS. THE REST IS MADE OF A WEE BIT OF DIRT, DUST MITE DEAD BODIES, AND DUST MITE POOPS.

- Right now in your bed there are millions of dust mites, and each one poops about twenty times a day.

- Dust mites eat the dead skin flakes that have fallen off of your body. So yummy!

- Most people who have allergies to dust are actually reacting to the dust mites.

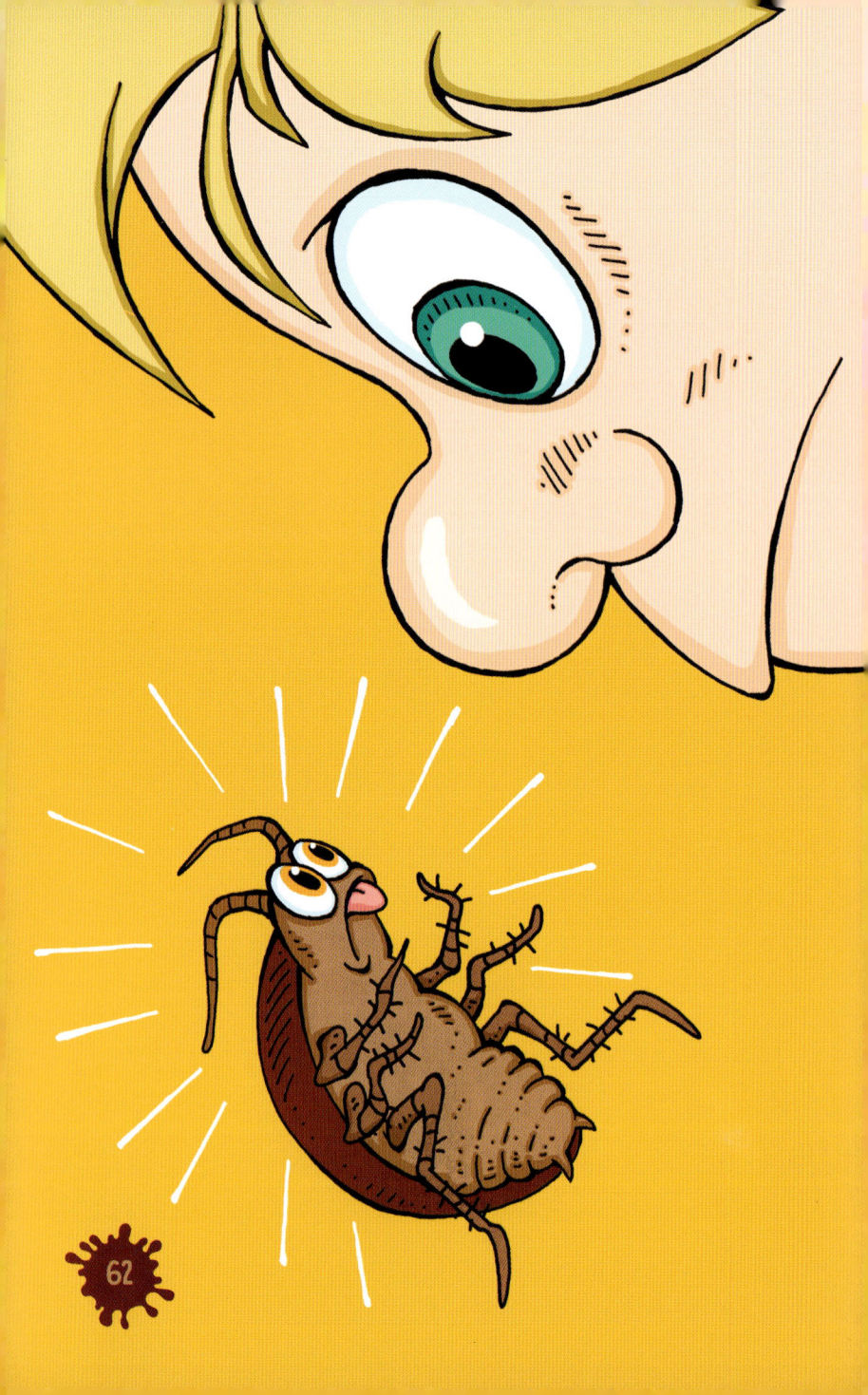

COCKROACHES

COCKROACHES THINK HUMANS ARE SO DISGUSTING, THEY WILL LICK THEMSELVES CLEAN AFTER A HUMAN TOUCH.

- A male and female German cockroach can result in 500,000 cockroaches after one year. An Asian cockroach couple would result in ten million roaches after one year.

- Cockroach droppings and dribbles make a room smell musty.

- Cockroaches eat pretty much anything, but they really like cinnamon rolls, white bread, and boiled potatoes.

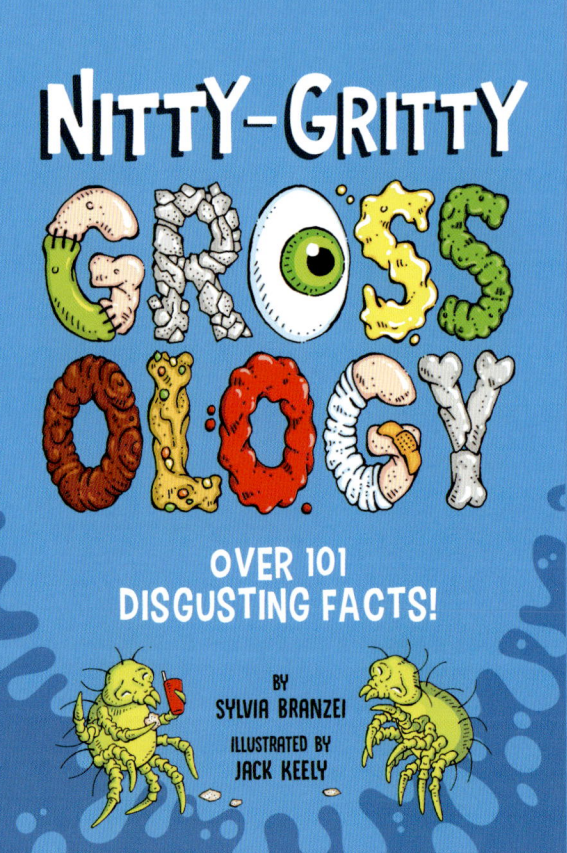